And to All
a Good Night

Christmas Folklore

W

North American Folklore for Youth

An Apple a Day: Folk Proverbs and Riddles

And to All a Good Night: Christmas Folklore

Black Cats and White Wedding Dresses: Folk Customs

Campfire Songs, Ballads, and Lullabies: Folk Music

Celebrations Throughout the Year: Holiday Folklore

Heroes, Fools, and Ghosts: Folk Tales and Legends

Quilts, Rag Dolls, and Rocking Chairs: Folk Arts and Crafts

Sirens and Smoke: Firefighters' Folklore

Tell Me a Story: Family Folklore

You're It! Tag, Red Rover, and Other Folk Games

And to All
a Good Night

Christmas Folklore

Bill Palmer

Mason Crest

Mason Crest
370 Reed Road
Broomall, Pennsylvania 19008
www.masoncrest.com

Printed and bound in the United States of America.

First printing
9 8 7 6 5 4 3 2 1

Library of Congress Cataloging-in-Publication Data

Palmer, Bill, 1957-
 And to all a good night : christmas folklore / Bill Palmer.
    p. cm.
 Includes index.
 ISBN 978-1-4222-2487-8 (hardcover) — ISBN 978-1-4222-2486-1
(hardcover series) — ISBN 978-1-4222-9252-5 (ebook)
 1. Christmas—Folklore. I. Title.
 GT4985.5.P35 2012
 394.2663—dc23

                              2012013559

Produced by Harding House Publishing Services, Inc.
www.hardinghousepages.com
Cover design by Torque Advertising + Design.

Contents

 Introduction

by Dr. Alan Jabbour

What do a story, a joke, a fiddle tune, a quilt, a dance, a game of jacks, a holiday celebration, and a Halloween costume have in common? Not much, at first glance. But they're all part of the stuff we call "folklore."

The word "folklore" means the ways of thinking and acting that are learned and passed along by ordinary people. Folklore goes from grandparents to parents to children—and on to *their* children. It may be passed along in words, like the urban legend we hear from friends who promise us that it *really* happened to someone they know. Or it may be tunes or dance steps we pick up on the block where we live. It could be the quilt our aunt made. Much of the time we learn folklore without even knowing where or how we learned it.

Folklore is not something that's far away or long ago. It's something we use and enjoy every day! It is often ordinary—

and yet at the same time, it makes life seem very special. Folklore is the culture we share with others in our homes, our neighborhoods, and our places of worship. It helps tell us who we are.

Our first sense of who we are comes from our families. Family folklore—like eating certain meals together or prayers or songs—gives us a sense of belonging. But as we grow older we learn to belong to other groups as well. Maybe your family is Irish. Or maybe you live in a Hispanic neighborhood in New York City. Or you might live in the country in the middle of Iowa. Maybe you're a Catholic—or a Muslim—or you're Jewish. Each one of these groups to which you belong will have it's own folklore. A certain dance step may be African American. A story may have come from Germany. A hymn may be Protestant. A recipe may have been handed down by your Italian grandmother. All this folklore helps the people who belong to a certain group feel connected to each other.

Folklore can make each group special, different from all the others. But at the same time folklore is one of the best ways we can get to know to each other. We can learn about Vietnamese immigrants by eating Vietnamese foods. We can understand newcomers from Somalia by enjoying their music and dance. Stories, songs, and artwork move from group to group. And everyone is the richer!

Folklore isn't something you usually learn in school. Somebody, somewhere, taught you that jump-rope rhyme you know—but you probably can't remember *who* taught you. You definitely didn't learn it in a schoolbook, though! You can study folklore and learn about it—that's what you are doing now in this book!—but folklore normally is something that just gets passed along from person to person.

This series of books explores the many kinds folklore you can find across the North American continent. As you read, you'll learn something about yourself—and you'll learn about your neighbors as well!

✳ ONE
What Is Christmas?

Words to Understand

Something that is *commercial* has to do with businesses making money.

The *solstice* is when the sun reaches the highest point in the sky as seen from either the North Pole or the South Pole. There are two solstices each year. One is the beginning of winter in December, and the other is the beginning of summer in June.

A *tradition* is the way something has been done for a long time. It's been passed down from grandparents to parents to their children—and one day, children will pass it on to their children and grandchildren.

Christmas is a very old holiday. It has been celebrated in a lot of ways for many years. The way we celebrate Christmas today is very different from how we celebrated 500 years ago. Or even just 100 years ago.

Christmas started out as a Christian holiday. For many people, this day still celebrates the birth of Jesus. It's an important part of the religious year.

For other people today, Christmas isn't a very religious holiday. It's more about giving gifts. It's about celebrating family.

Of course, Christmas has also become very **commercial**. People spend a lot of money on presents. There are advertisements on every TV channel.

Children love the magic of Christmas morning!

Most everyone around the world knows about Christmas. But the holiday has a lot of different roots. Here are some of them.

Ancient Days

The shortest day of the year is on December 21. It's the beginning of winter. That day is called the *solstice*. The night is very long.

Early people were afraid when nights grew long and days grew short. They worried the sun would never come back. Maybe it would be dark forever.

On the day when the days finally began to get longer, people celebrated. They lit torches and candles. They had feasts and games. Rich people gave gifts to poor people.

Today, some of these things are still important in modern Christmas. We light candles and decorate our houses with lights. We eat a lot. We might play games.

Romans

Christianity was new about 2,000 years ago. It grew and grew during the time the Roman Empire spread over much of what is today Europe. When Christianity was new, another religion competed with it.

Some Romans believed in a god called Mithra. His birth was on December 25. Sound familiar? Mithra was actually a lot like

Jesus. That was one reason early Christians decided that Jesus's birthday was on December 25 too.

Christianity

We think of Christmas as a Christian holiday. After all, Christians follow Jesus Christ. Christians all over the world celebrate his birth at Christmas.

The traditional Christmas story tells about how Jesus was born. People tell this story in churches today. Or they set up nativity scenes with everyone in the story—the angels, Mary and Joseph, the animals, the shepherds, the Wise Men, and of course, the Baby Jesus.

The Christmas story starts with an angel. The Angel Gabriel came to a young girl named Mary and told her she was going to have a special baby, a baby who would bring God's love to the world. That baby was Jesus.

Mary and her husband Joseph had to travel to Bethlehem, but the city was so crowded they couldn't find a place to stay. They ended up staying in a stable, where animals like cows and donkeys stayed. While they were there, Jesus was born. Mary made a bed for him in the manger, where the cows' hay was put for them to eat.

Meanwhile, more angels came to some shepherds who were watching their sheep in the fields outside of Bethlehem. The

The nativity scene is a common Christmas decoration.

angels told the shepherds about Jesus—and the shepherds came running to see this special baby.

Wise men from faraway lands learned about Jesus from studying the sky. They saw a star that led them to the home where Jesus was living with Mary and Joseph. They brought with them gifts to give the little boy.

All the characters in the story became important to Christmas folklore. From the animals to the angels, from the shepherds to the Wise Men, they all became part of the story that people told over and over.

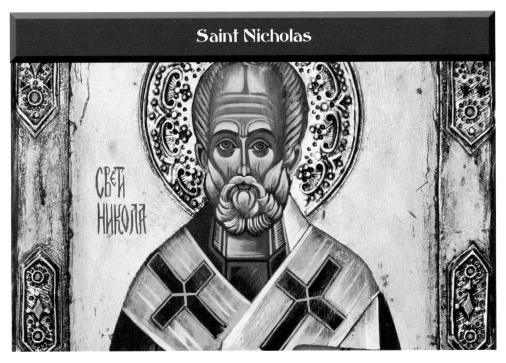

Saint Nicholas

Over the centuries, the story of Jesus' birth has been told in many languages. People used songs, poems, plays, and paintings to tell the old story. All these have become part of our folklore today. They're part of how we understand the world, information that we didn't have to learn in school because instead we learned it from our parents and grandparents, from our brothers and sisters and our friends.

Saint Nicholas

Today Santa Claus has become almost as important to Christmas folklore as the Baby Jesus. We have lots of stories about Santa Claus, and every year, these stories are told again, sometimes in new ways in movies and books.

But the first Santa Claus story was told long, long ago about a real man, who was named Nicholas. Nicholas was a follower of Jesus Christ. He loved other people and did his best to give to everyone around him. He became famous because of all the gifts he had given people. People told stories about him.

One day, says one of these stories, Nicholas heard that a man was going to sell his daughter into slavery. Nicholas didn't like that. He collected a bag of gold. Then he tossed the bag through the chimney and crept away.

The story says that the man's daughter had washed her socks the night before. She hung them by the fire to dry. The gold that Nicholas threw down the chimney landed in the socks.

In the end, the man didn't sell his daughter. He had enough money now to pay his debts.

Does any of this sound familiar? Think about it! We hang stockings by the fire. We give gifts. Santa Claus's gifts come down the chimney.

As more and more stories were told about Saint Nicholas, the man who lived a long time ago, he gradually started to look a lot like the Santa Claus we know today!

But Santa Claus isn't the only *tradition* that makes Christmas the way it is today. There are a lot of familiar Christmas traditions. All of them help give us that Christmassy feeling. They're part of Christmas folklore.

✳ TWO
Christmas Animals

> **Words to Understand**
>
> A *caravan* is a group of people and animals that travel together across the desert.
>
> *Immigrants* are people who leave their homelands and go to another country to live.

Because Jesus was born in a stable—really, a barn—animals played an important role in the Christmas story. Then the angels came to sing to shepherds who were watching their sheep. And then there were the Wise Men and their camels. All those animals captured people's imaginations. Over the years, more stories were told about Christmas animals.

The Christmas Camel

Before the Wise Men brought their gifts to baby Jesus, they had to buy camels. They wanted to get there quickly after all.

The Wise Men bought a mother camel and a baby. Nobody spotted the tiny camel among the many bags and bundles. The Wise Men had been traveling for many days before they noticed him.

The baby camel had a hard time keeping up with the *caravan*. The little camel tripped and stumbled. He was almost left behind in a town. He fell farther and farther behind.

Eventually, the baby camel caught up to his mother. Everyone had come to a stop in front of a stable. Everyone was kneeling.

The little camel tripped again. He felt a small hand touch his forehead. A little voice said, "You have worked so hard to follow your mother through the desert. You will share my blessings with all children as a reward."

From then on, the camel worked to spread the love of Jesus. He brings presents to children at Christmas to this day.

WHY CAMELS?

Camels were originally tamed by traders going from southern Arabia to the northern Middle East. Although the Bible doesn't actually say that the Wise Men rode on camels, it makes sense that they would have. Camels can carry heavy loads up to almost 1,000 pounds. They can also travel over long distances at speeds of 25 miles a day. What's more, these beasts are able to go about a week without food and water. They can lose one-fourth of their body weight without getting sick. Camels were the main source of transportation in the desert, and the camel became a sign of wealth in the ancient world.

The Christmas Lamb

Many flocks of sheep grazed on the hills above Bethlehem, including two lambs. They loved to listen to the shepherds talk. One day, a very old shepherd was talking about a child who would be born to poor parents but would become a king. He told them that this was an important person. He also said that there would be a sign when the child was born.

The lambs were excited. Shepherds were poor, so they wondered if one of the shepherds' babies would be the king. They waited for the sign.

As they watched and listened, nothing happened. Finally the smaller lamb said, "You can't find anything unless you look for it. Not even grass. Let's go look for the child."

So the two small lambs began their search. First they looked into every hut and explored the fires where shepherds kept watch. But they did not find the baby. They continued along the road between the hills until they arrived at the road to Bethlehem.

As the two sheep walked, the larger lamb complained that they were foolish to keep going. He lay down to sleep.

"You stay here and sleep," said the other lamb. "But I am going to keep looking."

As the smaller lamb traveled, he looked up in the sky. Suddenly, he saw a burst of light and heard the song of angels. He knew this was the sign he had been seeking. He followed the light to a ramshackle barn on the edge of Bethlehem.

The lamb could hear cows mooing inside the barn. When he entered, he saw a baby lying on a pile of hay. The lamb knelt beside the child and nuzzled his tiny hands. Then he said to the baby, "You and I will remember that a small lamb was the first to find you, the Christ Child."

Turning Stories into Folklore

The camel story is a story from Syria. *Immigrants* brought the story with them when they came to live in the United States.

In some Syrian families, a camel leaves presents instead of Santa Claus.

The story of the lamb is a folktale told by Christians who lived in the Middle East. They too brought the story with them when they moved to other parts of the world.

People just naturally make new stories around other stories. They use their imaginations to picture what things were like. They also paint pictures and make up songs. And all this gets passed along from person to person, from parents to children. It turns into folklore.

Traditions are another kind of folklore. Many Christmas traditions have to do with animals. Families used to bring all their animals in the house on Christmas Eve. Some people believed that animals could talk at midnight on Christmas Eve—or that they would fall to their knees, remembering that first Christmas in the stable so long ago.

Many of today's Christmas animal stories have to do with reindeer. But reindeer weren't a part of the Christmas story until the nineteenth century when a man named Clement C. Moore wrote a poem. It was called "A Visit from Saint Nicholas" and it became part of our Christmas folklore.

'Twas the night before Christmas, when all through the house

Not a creature was stirring, not even a mouse;

The stockings were hung by the chimney with care,

In hopes that St. Nicholas soon would be there.

The children were nestled all snug in their beds,

While visions of sugar-plums danced in their heads;

And mamma in her 'kerchief, and I in my cap,

Had just settled down for a long winter's nap,

When out on the lawn there arose such a clatter,

I sprang from the bed to see what was the matter.

Away to the window I flew like a flash,

Tore open the shutters and threw up the sash.

The moon on the breast of the new-fallen snow,

Gave the luster of mid-day to objects below,

When, what to my wondering eyes should appear,

But a miniature sleigh, and eight tiny reindeer,

With a little old driver, so lively and quick,

I knew in a moment it must be St. Nick.

More rapid than eagles his coursers they came,

And he whistled, and shouted, and called them by name;

"Now, DASHER! now, DANCER! now, PRANCER and VIXEN!

On, COMET! on CUPID! on, DONNER and BLITZEN!

To the top of the porch! to the top of the wall!

Now dash away! dash away! dash away all!"

As dry leaves that before the wild hurricane fly,

When they meet with an obstacle, mount to the sky,

So up to the house-top the coursers they flew,

With the sleigh full of toys, and St. Nicholas too.

And then, in a twinkling, I heard on the roof

The prancing and pawing of each little hoof.

LET'S NOT FORGET RUDOLPH!

Rudolph the Red-Nosed Reindeer had also become an important animal in Christmas folklore. He first appeared in a 1939 booklet written by Robert L. May and published by Montgomery Ward.

CHRISTMAS GOATS?

In Finland, the Yule Goat was originally said to be an ugly creature that frightened children, and demanded gifts at Christmas. In other parts of Scandinavia, people thought of the Yule Goat as an invisible creature that would appear some time before Christmas to make sure that the Christmas preparations were done right. During the nineteenth century, the goat became the one who brought gifts. One of the men in the family would dress up as the Yule Goat. Nowadays, Scandinavians no longer have a goat that brings them presents at Christmastime, but a straw goat is still a common Christmas decoration in all of Scandinavia.

Almost every child in the world now knows that reindeer pull Santa's sleigh and deliver gifts to children.

Santa's reindeer aren't so different from those camels!

✳ THREE
Santa Claus

Santa Claus is good example of how folklore grows and spreads over the years. In the modern world, things like popular songs, books, and movies may add to the stories. But then people forget all about where the stories came from. They just pass them along. The new stories mix with the old stories. They're folklore.

Almost everyone knows this story. Santa Claus lives at the North Pole with his magical elves (who make toys all year long) and nine (including Rudolph) flying reindeer. According to a piece of folklore that started out with a 1934 song "Santa Claus Is Coming to Town," Santa Claus makes a list of children throughout the world. He puts them into "naughty" and "nice" categories. Then he brings presents, including toys and candy, to all of the well-behaved children in the world. Sometimes he brings coal to the naughty children. He does all this on the single night of Christmas Eve with the help of the reindeer who pull his sleigh.

Santa Claus sure has gone through many changes during the years. He's known in lots of different countries by different names. One thing is always true, though—Santa brings gifts and joy.

Remember the story of Saint Nicholas in chapter 1? He was kind and generous to everyone around him. He gave away money and food to the poor and to the church. A long time ago, people started giving gifts on Saint Nicholas Eve (December 6). They did this as a way to remember Saint Nicholas. The first people to do that were nuns in France. They left gifts at poor people's homes. The gifts were usually special foods like fruits and nuts.

Pretty soon, the tradition spread across Europe. In the Netherlands, children celebrated Saint Nicholas Day by putting wooden shoes beside the fireplace when they went to bed. When they woke up, "Sinterklaas" would have left little presents in their shoes. (Sinterklaas means "Saint Nicholas" in Dutch.)

Sinterklaas rode a white horse. He wore a red robe and hat. He also smoked a pipe. That sounds a lot like our Santa Claus.

In Germany, "Krist Kindle" visited kids. (Krist Kindle means Christ Child in German.) He brought gifts on Christmas Eve, December 24.

In Sweden, "Jultomten" brings gifts on a sleigh pulled by goats. In Ghana, Father Christmas delivers gifts out of the jungle. In Hawaii, he rides on a boat.

All of these stories from around the world combined into the Santa Claus you know today. He rides in a sleigh pulled by

Sinterklaas posing for pictures in the Netherlands.

reindeer. He visits on Christmas Eve. He wears red clothes and a hat. He has a white beard and he's very fat. He lives in the North Pole.

Today, Santa Claus continues to be a big part of Christmas. The holiday just wouldn't be the same without him!

A popular American tradition is leaving milk and cookies for the Christmas Eve visitor. In the morning, children wake to an empty glass and only crumbs on the plate . . . proof that Santa has been there.

❄ FOUR
Christmas Plants

Words to Understand

Symbolize means that something stands for an idea that might be harder to understand otherwise.

Purity means that something is all one thing, without being made dirty or diluted. So pure gold, for example, is all gold. It doesn't have anything else mixed up with it. Jesus was pure love, without selfishness or anything else mixed up in him the way most people have.

A *miracle* is something amazing and wonderful that can't be explained by science.

We celebrate Christmas during the winter. That's a time when green things stop growing. Animals sleep in their dens. There's not much life outside. But Christmas is all about life! We use a lot of plants to celebrate Christmas. Growing things have been a part of Christmas for a long time.

Christmas greens represent life. Long ago, the Romans decorated their homes with palm trees and evergreens in the winter. They gave each other green branches for good luck. Those ancient traditions are still showing up in the modern world. They're a part of our Christmas folklore.

Christmas Trees

The first plant that comes to mind when you think about Christmas is probably the Christmas tree!

Christmas trees first became a tradition about a thousand years ago in Europe. Like today, they were evergreen trees. People decorated them with apples and small cookies.

One story claims that Martin Luther started the Christmas tree tradition. Martin Luther was a famous religious man in Germany who lived a long time ago. He started new ways of thinking about Christianity.

According to the story, he was traveling home to his family one night. He looked up at the sky and saw the stars between an evergreen tree's branches. It reminded him of what the sky must have been like when Jesus was born.

He cut down a tree and took it home. Then he put candles on its branches. It was almost like putting stars on the tree. The tree in his house reminded him of Jesus.

Slowly, decorating trees became more popular. Lots of Germans did it. They put small gifts in the trees' branches.

Pinecones, cookies, fruits, and nuts all had their place in the green branches. So did little toys, baskets, candy, and candles. Then, in the eighteenth and nineteenth centuries, German immigrants brought the Christmas tree idea with them to the United States.

In the 1800s, people began putting angels on the tops of their trees. After trees caught on, even the President of the United States started putting up a tree. The White House had a tree. That's still an American tradition.

When your grandparents were children, they may have decorated their trees on Christmas Eve and taken them down 12 days later. Today, many people put up their trees the day after Thanksgiving and leave them up until New Year's.

Holly

Holly grows even in the winter. Its leaves don't fall off. That makes it a perfect plant for Christmas.

The ancient Celts in Europe liked holly. These people lived in parts of Europe hundreds and hundreds of years ago. Their ancestors still live in parts of Europe today. The Celts brought holly into their homes. Because it didn't die in the winter, it reminded the Celts of the life that never died, even in the winter.

Ancient Romans wore wreaths made of holly. The Roman god Saturn often wore holly. Today, our Santa Claus sometimes is shown wearing holly, just like Saturn.

In Christianity, holly is also an important plant. The white flowers in spring *symbolize* Jesus' *purity*. The red berries remind people of his blood. The leaves are like the crown of thorns he wore on the cross. The fact that they never die, even in the cold, reminds people that Jesus rose from the dead.

Mistletoe

Has anyone ever kissed you because you were standing under a bunch of mistletoe? Hanging this plant in a doorway is a Christmas tradition.

For the Celts, mistletoe symbolized strength and power. Today we think of mistletoe as a way to spread green cheer during Christmas. It's a pretty decoration—and a fun kissing tradition.

Mistletoe

A myth from northern Europe tells a story about mistletoe. Balder, the sun god, dreamed of his own death. His mother, Frigga, was scared. She begged the plants and animals to not hurt her son. Frigga forgot to ask the mistletoe.

Loki was the god of evil. He didn't like Balder. He made an arrow out of mistletoe. Balder was shot by the arrow and he died.

All the gods were sad. They all tried to bring him back to life. Frigga eventually did it. She was so happy that she cried. Her tears turned into mistletoe berries. She was so happy that she kissed every god that walked under the tree where the mistletoe grew.

Poinsettias

Poinsettias

When we think of Christmas, we think of the colors green and red. These colors once stood for the blood of Jesus and his life that never died. Today, we just think of red and green as part of the Christmas folklore we've always known.

The poinsettia plant has both of those colors. In Mexico, the poinsettia first became part of Christmas folklore. One legend says that the red and green plant came from a *miracle*. A poor child went to visit Jesus. He didn't have a gift. Instead, he picked some weeds. When he gave them to Jesus, the weeds turned into bright red flowers.

A man named Dr. Poinsett found these red plants when he was in Mexico. He sent them back to the United States. There, they became a part of Christmas.

Christmas carolers performing

✳ FIVE
Christmas Greetings: Song and Cards

Words to Understand

The earliest meaning of *tablet* was a flat slab of wood, stone, or clay that was used for writing by scratching letters into it. This early meaning is why today we talk about a "tablet of paper." It is also why we call certain computer devices intended for writing "tablets" as well!

When something is *mass-produced*, lots of it are made all at once. Most things you buy today are made this way, from clothes to cars. But it used to be that people made everything by hand, one at a time.

There is one more kind of Christmas folklore we haven't talked about yet: songs and greetings.

Christmas Music

Think about it. During the month of December, almost everywhere you go you hear Christmas songs. In the store. On the car radio. On television. Some of these songs are new. Some of them are a little older. And some of them are very, very old.

Singing and music have always been a part of celebrations. Music might be one of the very oldest Christmas traditions.

Christmas carols are some of the oldest holiday songs. We keep singing the same ones over and over. New songs never replace the old ones.

Music is an important part of the holidays.

Like stories, we pass carols down from generation to generation. Parents and teachers pass them on to kids. We don't really learn them from books. We learn by listening. You probably find yourself humming along sometimes. Someday you will pass this music on to your children. You will be part of the folk traditions that you learned when you were a child! You'll add a little bit to it along the way. That's the way folklore works. It just keeps growing and spreading.

Christmas Cards

Songs are one way to pass along the Christmas message to others. Another type of greeting and expression of happiness is the Christmas card. Writing greetings began a while ago. In ancient Rome, people exchanged clay **tablets** with good luck messages. They also gave each other coins with greetings. Now, we give each other cards. But the idea is the same.

In 1843, a man named Sir Henry Cole wanted to send greetings to his friends. He didn't have enough time to write them all by hand. He asked a friend to create a card. Then he could sign each card and send them to his friends. He sent out 1,000!

That was the first **mass-produced** Christmas card (though people sent handmade ones before). Now it's a Christmas tradition.

Joyce Hall

HALLMARK

In 1910, a man named Joyce Hall began selling picture postcards from two shoeboxes. By 1914, he replaced his postcards with greeting cards. After a big fire that destroyed all their cards, Hall and his brothers bought a company. The rest is history. You've probably received and sent Hallmark greeting cards many times!

Sometimes people complain that we've lost the true meaning of Christmas. But Christmas means different things to different people. For some people, it isn't a very religious holiday. Other people still focus more on the Christian religion. For them it's a time to think about Jesus and his birth. But for everyone, Christmas is a time to celebrate families. It's a time for giving and sharing. That's what Christmas has always meant. It is a time to think about love. It's a time to show others that we love them and to know that we are loved.

At Christmas time, we celebrate traditions that have been around for years. Christmas may have become a commercial holiday, a chance for businesses to make money by selling things. But it is still a folk celebration. And it's all those folk traditions that make Christmas so much fun!

Find Out More

In Books

Kelley, Emily. *Christmas Around the World.* Minneapolis, Minn.: Carolrhoda, 2004.

Lankford, Mary D. *Christmas Around the World.* New York: HarperCollins, 2008.

Morrison, Dorothy. *Yule: A Celebration of Light and Warmth.* Woodbury, Minn.: Llewellyn, 2000.

Oppenheim, Joanne. *The Miracle of the First Poinsettia.* Cambridge, Mass.: Barefoot Books, 2003.

Palmer, Bill. *Santa Claus.* Vestal, N.Y.: Anamchara Books, 2012.

Stevens, Beth. *Celebrate Christmas Around the World.* Westminster, Calif.: Teacher Created Resources, 2003.

On the Internet

Christmas Folk Stories
americanfolklore.net/folklore/christmas-stories

Christmas History, Traditions, and Folklore
urbanlegends.about.com/od/christmaslore/Christmas.htm

Christmas Tree: Legends, Traditions, History
www.ewtn.com/library/chistory/xmastree.htm

History of Santa Claus: Legends, Folklore, and Traditions
www.mountainelves.com/Folklore/legends.html

Index

Picture Credits

About the Author and the Consultant

Bill Palmer is an author and editor who has always loved Christmas. He is especially interested in the folklore and history of Santa Claus. He has given talks and written a book on this topic.

Dr. Alan Jabbour is a folklorist who served as the founding director of the American Folklife Center at the Library of Congress from 1976 to 1999. Previously, he began the grant-giving program in folk arts at the National Endowment for the Arts (1974-76). A native of Jacksonville, Florida, he was trained at the University of Miami (B.A.) and Duke University (M.A., Ph.D.). A violinist from childhood on, he documented old-time fiddling in the Upper South in the 1960s and 1970s. A specialist in instrumental folk music, he is known as a fiddler himself, an art he acquired directly from elderly fiddlers in North Carolina, Virginia, and West Virginia. He has taught folklore and folk music at UCLA and the University of Maryland and has published widely in the field.